A Note to Parents and Teachers

DK READERS is a compelling programme for beginning readers, designed in conjunction with literacy experts, including Maureen Fernandes, B.Ed (Hons). Maureen has spent many years teaching literacy, both in the classroom and as a consultant in schools.

Beautiful illustrations and superb full-colour photographs combine with engaging, easy-to-read stories to offer a fresh approach to each subject in the series.

Each DK READER is guaranteed to capture a child's interest while developing his or her reading skills, general knowledge and love of reading.

The five levels of DK READERS are aimed at different reading abilities, enabling you to choose the books that are exactly right for your child:

Pre-level 1: Learning to read

Level 1: Beginning to read

Level 2: Beginning to read alone

Level 3: Reading alone

Level 4: Proficient readers

The "normal" age at which a child begins to read can be anywhere from three to eight years old. Adult participation through the lower levels is very helpful for providing encouragement, discussing storylines and sounding out unfamiliar words.

No matter which level you select, you can be sure that you are helping your child learn to read, then read to learn!

LONDON, NEW YORK, MUNICH,
MELBOURNE AND DELHI

Created by Tall Tree Ltd
Editor Kate Simkins
Designer Jonathan Vipond

Senior Editor Lindsay Kent
Senior Art Editor Rob Perry
Publishing Manager Simon Beecroft
Category Publisher Alex Allan
DTP Designer Hanna Ländin
Production Nick Seston

Reading Consultant
Maureen Fernandes

This edition published in 2014
First published in Great Britain in 2007 by
Dorling Kindersley Limited,
80 Strand, London WC2E 0RL
A Penguin Random House Company

10 9 8 7 6 5 4 3 2
002-277244-Sept/14

A CIP record for this book is available from the British Library.

ISBN 978-1-40532-010-8

High resolution workflow by Media Development and Printing
Ltd, UK.
Printed and bound in China

marvel.com
© 2014 MARVEL

Discover more at
www.dk.com

Contents

4   Who are the
    Fantastic Four?

6   Origins of the
    Fantastic Four

10 Underground enemy

12 Mr Fantastic

16 The Invisible Woman

20 The Human Torch

24 The Thing

28 Fantastic technology

32 Amazing allies

34 Stand-in members

36 Awesome adversaries

46 Earth's protectors

48 Glossary

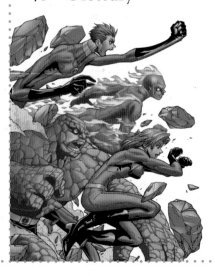

DK READERS

READING 3 ALONE

MARVEL
FANTASTIC FOUR

The World's Greatest Superteam

Written by Neil Kelly

Who are the Fantastic Four?

The Fantastic Four is a Super Hero team with amazing powers. Each member has a different power.

The Thing has superhuman strength and a craggy, super-tough body. Mr Fantastic has the ability to stretch his body like a rubber band. The Invisible Woman can make herself invisible and create force fields. The Human Torch can turn his body into flames. The team uses its powers to protect Earth from Super Villains and evil aliens.

The Fantastic Four are, from left to right, the Thing, Mr Fantastic, the Invisible Woman and the Human Torch.

Origins of the Fantastic Four

The Fantastic Four gained their special abilities in a space accident. They took their new starship on a test flight but were bombarded by cosmic rays. The rays broke through the ship's shields and changed their bodies forever.

The Fantastic Four's starship was caught in a radiation storm.

Sue Storm turned invisible after absorbing the cosmic rays.

Each member now had special abilities. Sue Storm was the first to show her new powers. She suddenly disappeared before everyone's eyes. Then her brother Johnny became hotter and hotter until he burst into flames.

Johnny Storm became the Human Torch.

Ben Grimm was the next to change.
His skin became orange and rock-like,
and he gained amazing strength.
Ben was unhappy with his new
appearance and called himself the Thing
because he no longer looked human.

*Ben changed into
a scaly, orange monster
called the Thing.*

Fantastic Four, Inc.
The Fantastic Four set up
a business – Fantastic Four,
Inc. – based in New York City,
USA. The profits made from
Reed's inventions meant they
could offer their services for free.

Finally, Reed Richards, the team's
leader, discovered he could now stretch
his limbs like a piece of elastic.

The friends named themselves
the Fantastic Four (FF for short) and
promised to use their abilities to do good.

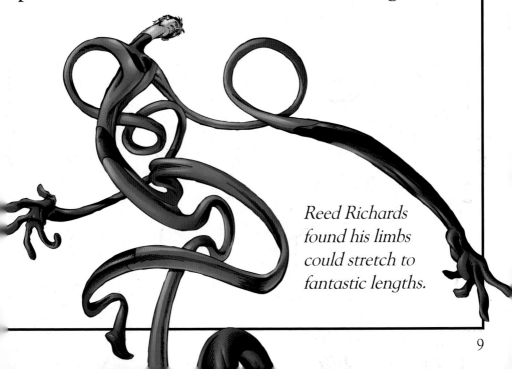

*Reed Richards
found his limbs
could stretch to
fantastic lengths.*

9

Underground enemy

The first enemy the Fantastic Four faced was the Mole Man. He ruled the underground kingdom of Subterranea (SUB-TER-RAIN-E-UH) and hated humans. The Mole Man was almost blind, but he possessed a radar sense that enabled him to find his way around.

The Mole Man discovered a cave on a mysterious island that led to the underground world of Subterranea.

The Mole Man planned to steal the world's atomic power plants and use his army of monsters to take over the planet.

The Fantastic Four use their powers to defeat one of the Mole Man's terrifying giant monsters.

Mr Fantastic

Reed Richards – also known
as Mr Fantastic – is
a scientific genius.
He was a child
prodigy and was
taking college-
level courses by the age of
14. Reed's mental abilities
are matched only
by his physical powers.

   Mr Fantastic can bend,
squash or expand his body
into any solid shape.

*Mr Fantastic can extend his body to
incredible lengths, but the farther
he stretches the weaker he becomes.*

He can spread
his body out like
a living parachute or even
turn himself into a human
tent! Reed's special powers
mean he can flatten himself so
that he is as thin as paper or make
himself slim enough to pass through
the eye of a needle.

*Reed can stretch
his neck, torso
and limbs up to
500 metres
(1,500 feet).*

Reed's flexible body gives him
an advantage in his fights against
Super Villains. He also invents incredible
new machines and devices that the FF
use in their missions. Gadgets such as
Reed's power-packed electronic
knuckle-dusters enable him to knock out
tough opponents
like Annihilus
(AN-I-HILL-US)
with ease.

*Annihilus feels
the force of
Mr Fantastic's
power-assisted
punch.*

Mr Fantastic is married to Sue Storm, the Invisible Woman. They have a son, Franklin, named after Sue's father.

Reed, Sue and Franklin.

Mr Fantastic's flexible body can absorb bullets and shells and catapult them back at his enemies.

The Invisible Woman

The Invisible Woman
has many special
abilities. As well as
being able to make
herself invisible,
Sue Richards can
shield people or
objects so they can't
be seen. She can also
project invisible, super-
strong force fields
using her mind.

*At first, Sue called herself
the Invisible Girl. She later
changed her name to
the Invisible Woman.*

Sue designed the FF's smart, blue uniforms.

Sue can even fly, keeping herself airborne on a column of mental energy.

She is the peacemaker of the Fantastic Four, solving arguments when the other members fall out.

To stop a squabble between the other members of the FF going too far, Sue surrounds the Thing with an invisible force field.

Sue Storm first met
Reed Richards on
a trip to New York City
when she was 12 years old.
Reed was a university
student who was staying
with Sue's aunt.

Years later, Sue met
Reed again and they fell in love.
After they got married, she changed
her name to Sue Richards.

*The Invisible Woman
can use her force fields
to create solid shapes
like this speedy,
transparent bobsleigh.*

Sue's mental powers are amazing. She can make fearsome weapons, such as these invisible grappling hooks, just by imagining them.

When Reed was about to launch his new starship, Sue insisted that she and her brother Johnny join the crew.

Hate not love
The villain Hate-Monger briefly transformed Sue into Malice (MA-LISS), an evil enemy of the FF. Sue is a loving, caring person, but Malice was full of hatred.

The Human Torch

Cosmic rays turned Johnny
Storm into the Human Torch,
giving him the power to
generate super-heated flames
from any part of his body.
Johnny is also able to fly,
carried by the hot gases
created by his flames. He can
direct deadly fireballs at
his enemies and can release
all of his body's energy in
a huge "nova-burst" explosion.

When he turns on the heat,
Johnny can often be heard to
cry, "Flame on!"

*Johnny's fiery powers
allow him to soar
through the skies.*

Johnny is a daring driver and a skilled mechanic. His flashiness and good looks annoy Ben Grimm, who thinks he is a show-off. The pair are very competitive and squabble all the time.

When Johnny and Ben fight the FF's enemies, their rivalry is forgotten.

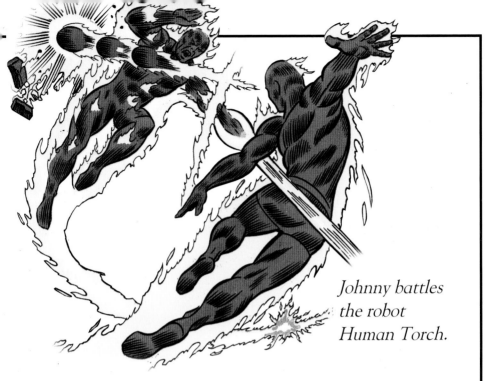

Johnny battles the robot Human Torch.

Johnny once fought another Human Torch. The other Human Torch was a robot who battled against crime in the 1940s and 50s. He was reactivated and attacked Johnny.

Alicia and Johnny

Ben was upset when Johnny fell in love with his girlfriend Alicia Masters. But she turned out to be a Skrull agent in disguise named Lyja (LIE-JAR) – the real Alicia had been kidnapped.

The Thing

Ben Grimm's monstrous appearance earned him his FF name – the Thing. He has superhuman strength and a tough skin made up of heavy, orange scales.

The Thing does not need a special suit to survive in space or the depths of the ocean.

Ben met Reed Richards when they were roommates at university.

Ben Grimm, alias the Thing, leaps into action.

Ben can withstand armour-piercing shells and extremes of heat and cold. He also has a great sense of humour. When it's time to fight the bad guys, he's always ready with his favourite catchphrase – "it's clobberin' time!"

The Thing's powers are both a gift and a curse. Ben is not happy with the way he looks, but he is unable to change back to human form permanently. He has sometimes returned to normal, either by accident or through Reed Richards' experiments, but the effects do not usually last long.

Ben changes back to human form.

Ben has fought the Hulk many times. The green giant is bigger and stronger than the Thing, but Ben is more stubborn and determined.

Ben enjoys his work with the Fantastic Four – the world always needs "the ever-lovin' blue-eyed Thing!"

Fantastic technology

The FF's first headquarters was on the top five floors of the Baxter Building in New York City. Many of Reed Richards' most amazing inventions were built there, including the first Fantasti-car.

The first Fantasti-car was nicknamed "the flying bathtub" and could be used as a team vehicle or split into four separate flying machines.

When the Baxter Building was catapulted into space by Doctor Doom's heir, Kristoff Vernard, the FF built Four Freedoms Plaza in its place. This 45-storey building was later destroyed and a new version of the Baxter Building was created.

The second Baxter Building was built in space and teleported to Earth.

Many of Reed's inventions are
designed to help the FF defend Earth.
He has created flying vehicles, intelligent
robots, super-computers and even
thought projectors.

The Fantastic Four sometimes make
use of alien technology, such as
the captured Skrull starship that they use
for space travel. The team also have
a special sleigh that enables the FF to
travel through time.

*The new Fantasti-car is designed for long-range
missions. It is fitted with bulletproof windshields and
can travel much faster than the old Fantasti-car.*

Robot friend
Reed built a robot to assist him. He called it HERBIE, which stands for "Humanoid Experimental Robot B-Type Integrated Electronics"!

For quick trips, the FF use their four-person air-jet cycle.

Amazing allies

The Fantastic Four have many
Super Hero friends. When Sue and Reed
threw a party to celebrate their
engagement, the X-Men and
the Avengers were invited.

Other heroes who came along to wish
them luck included Professor X, Angel,
Captain America and Iron Man.

*Many Super Hero friends
joined the party.*

Caledonia is an expert swordswoman.

Postman hero

Willy Lumpkin was the FF's postman for many years. He has no special powers apart from the ability to wiggle his ears! He is a friend to the FF and even saved them from the criminal mastermind, the Mad Thinker.

Alysande Stuart, also known as Caledonia, works for the FF as Franklin's nanny. She is the champion of ancient Scotland.

Stand-in members

Unlike other Super Hero groups,
the Fantastic Four still has the same
team-mates. The original members
of the FF have left the group for short
periods, but always returned.
Others, including Ant-Man,
the She-Hulk, Power Man and Crystal,
have taken their place for a time.

When the Skrull De'Lila held the FF
hostage, everyone believed that they had
been killed. Super Heroes Spider-Man,
Ghost Rider, the Hulk and Wolverine
formed the All New Fantastic Four.
They discovered that the old FF were still
alive and freed them.

*The All New Fantastic Four are, from top
to bottom, Spider-Man (who is not wearing
his spider costume), the Hulk, Ghost Rider
and Wolverine.*

Awesome adversaries

The FF have faced many deadly foes. Doctor Doom is one of their greatest enemies. He is the ruler of Latveria, a small country in Eastern Europe.

Doom is a skilled scientist and inventor, who first met Reed Richards at university in New York. He uses his abilities to further his dream of ruling the world, but his plans are always foiled by the Fantastic Four.

Reed Richards and Doctor Doom trade blows.

Model-making villain

The Puppet Master creates life-like puppets out of special radioactive clay. When he makes a puppet of someone, the clay gives him the power to control them. His daughter, Alicia, is Ben's girlfriend.

Another villain, Ulysses Klaw (U-LISS-EZE CLAW), is able to change sound into physical objects. He can also create sounds that are loud enough to shatter steel.

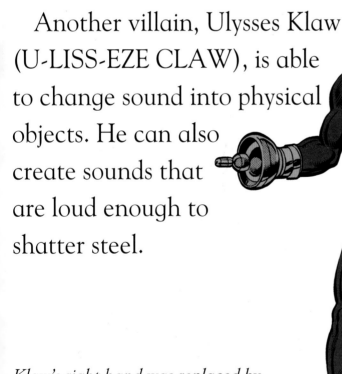

Klaw's right hand was replaced by a sonic blaster when Sue Richards shattered his real hand.

The Skrulls are an alien race of shape-changers. They can take on the appearance of any person, animal or thing. They have conquered hundreds of worlds by disguising themselves as the natives of a planet before attacking them.

Skrull agents impersonated the Fantastic Four and tried to turn the world against them, but the FF defeated them.

A Skrull agent turns back to normal after disguising himself as Reed.

The Skrulls and the Kree have one thing in common – they both hate the human race.

The Kree are the Skrulls' oldest enemies. The two races have been at war for thousands of years. The Kree are twice as strong as humans. They are ruled by a super-computer called the Supreme Intelligence.

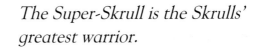

The Super-Skrull is the Skrulls' greatest warrior.

The Frightful Four are a group of Super Villains who joined forces to defeat a common enemy – the Fantastic Four. Their combined powers helped them to take control of the Baxter Building and hold the FF captive. Their plan was foiled, but they have since hatched many more evil plots and schemes.

The original Frightful Four were, from left to right, Madam Medusa, the Wizard, Trapster and Sandman. Over the years, the members have changed, but they always use their super-powers to try to defeat the Fantastic Four.

The super-strong robot Quasimodo can project power blasts from its left eye.

The criminal mastermind known as the Mad Thinker is a computer expert. He planned to seize control of New York City. While the FF were away, he broke into the Baxter Building and used Reed's research to make a powerful robot called Quasimodo. But the FF returned unexpectedly, and the Mad Thinker was defeated.

The Mad Thinker outsmarted the law for years – until he met the Fantastic Four.

Galactus, the Eater of Planets, is a terrifying enemy. He needs a special type of energy to survive, which can only be found on certain planets. Countless civilisations have been destroyed to satisfy his hunger.

When Galactus attacked Earth, the FF defeated him by threatening to destroy not only Galactus but also the whole Universe!

Galactus can teleport objects across the galaxy and create super-strong force fields.

The Silver Surfer turned against Galactus when the planet-eater threatened Earth. The Surfer believed that humanity was worth saving.

The alien Norrin Radd saved his homeworld from Galactus by becoming Galactus's herald. Galactus covered Radd's body with an indestructible silver coating and gave him a cosmic surf board so he could travel through space. Radd became the Silver Surfer and spent many years seeking out worlds for his master to eat.

The villain Annihilus wears an armoured suit that gives him amazing strength and allows him to fly at super-fast speeds. His Cosmic Control Rod fires deadly energy blasts and has stopped him aging. Annihlius believes he must destroy all other beings to stop them from stealing the Rod.

Annihilus can use cosmic energy to transform one object into another.

The super-powerful being Beyonder captured Earth's greatest heroes and villains and transported them to Battleworld. There, the FF were forced to fight enemies such as Doctor Doom.

In human form, Beyonder appears as a tall, dark-haired man.

Psycho-Man is so small that he cannot be seen by humans. He uses a mind-ray to fill his victims' minds with feelings of fear, doubt and hate.

Psycho-Man wears human-sized battle suits on Earth.

Earth's protectors

The Fantastic Four have faced many dangers together and defeated many enemies. Their greatest strength is that they are a family. Although they sometimes disagree or argue, they always sort out their differences.

The FF are always ready to defend Earth, and they continue to use their skills to make important discoveries in science and exploration.

With their amazing abilities and boundless courage, the Fantastic Four will always be the world's greatest superteam.

The Fantastic Four are ready to protect humanity from any threat.

Glossary

agents
Spies.

atomic
To do with atoms, the tiny particles of which things are made.

cosmic
Something that comes from outer space.

curse
A cause of bad luck.

energy
Power obtained from various sources. Humans get energy from food.

force fields
Invisible barriers around objects.

generate
Make.

genius
Someone who is much cleverer than most people.

herald
Someone who brings news.

indestructible
Impossible to damage or destroy.

knuckle-dusters
Metal coverings worn over the knuckles (finger joints) and used as weapons.

limbs
Arms and legs.

mental
To do with the mind.

missions
Duties or tasks.

natives
The people who were born in a place.

parachute
A large cloth that opens to slow down the fall of someone who jumps from a high place.

physical
To do with the body.

prodigy
An amazingly talented child.

profits
Money made from a business.

projectors
Machines for showing images.

radar
A machine that sends out radiowaves to work out the position of an object.

radiation
Rays of energy.

radioactive
Giving off energy.

reactivated
Made to work again.

rivalry
The act of trying to do better than someone else.

shells
Hollow cases filled with explosives that are fired from guns.

shields
Barriers that protect objects or people from harm.

sonic
To do with sound.

teleport
Move instantly from one place to another.

torso
The upper body except the head and arms.